THE OFFICIAL
WEST BROMWICH ALBION
FOOTBALL CLUB
ANNUAL 2014

Written by Dave Bowler
Designed by Iain Donnachie

A Grange Publication

Pictures © Laurie Rampling, AMA Sports Photography, Paul Bradbury

ISBN: 978-1-908925-52-7

£7.99

CONTENTS

It wasn't exactly a question of "Steve who?" when Steve Clarke took over as Albion's Head Coach in the summer of 2012, because he already had bags of experience as a coach at Liverpool, Newcastle, West Ham and, most of all, Chelsea.

STEVE CLARKE

But he had never been the man in charge before, always working as an assistant to big names like Jose Mourinho, Kenny Dalglish, Sir Bobby Robson and Gianfranco Zola. How would he handle the big time?

Easy!

Steve's Albion were too much for all comers across the first half of the 2012/13 season as he took the Throstles to third place in the Premier League by the end of November. There were more memorable days after that, including a 2-0 win at Anfield and that

amazing 5-5 draw against Manchester United on the final day of the 2012/13 season.

In the end, Albion finished in eighth place with 49 points, both Premier League records for the club. Nobody is saying "Steve who?" now! ∎

THE ALBION MAZE

It's a long way from one end of The Hawthorns to the other, especially when somebody has let the grass grow into a maze!

Can you help Shane Long find his way from his own goal to the opposition's – so that he can score the winner!

Answer on page 61.

SEASON REVIEW 2012-2013

2012/13, what a season that was! It opened at The Hawthorns with the arrival of the Premier League's newest addition to management, Steve Clarke, and ended at our home with the departure of the greatest manager ever – Sir Alex Ferguson.

Albion did the double over Liverpool, QPR and Southampton, put one over on the new United boss, saw off our old friend the Chelsea gaffer as well as Martin O'Neill, scored some great goals, watched some terrific performances, enjoyed our ups, felt deflated by our downs and ended up with our best ever Premier League points total and that amazing 5-5 finale. It's not quite the greatest story ever told, but it's a decent yarn nonetheless.

Over to Steve Clarke to tell us all about it!   >

Joining Albion, it was all very sudden. I'd just been informed by Liverpool that they were going to make a change and I was out of work. I got a phone call from Albion, we had a little chat and I came for an interview. Obviously, the first interview went well, there was a second one and after that, I was fortunate enough to get the job.

As an outsider looking in, the team was very well disciplined, very, very well organised and quite determined. I'd been at Liverpool the previous season and West Brom had come to Anfield and recorded a famous win. When you saw the game that afternoon, although Liverpool had a lot of possession, a lot of chances, the determination and the sheer willpower of West Bromwich Albion was impressive, with enough quality to win the game as well.

First impressions in pre-season were really favourable. I think when a new coach comes in, players respond no matter

what the circumstances are, they've got someone different, someone they don't know and I think all the players feel that they have to impress, so the start of the pre-season was great. I had a lot of the younger boys involved and between them and the senior boys, there was a good mix and everybody impressed early in pre-season which was great because it gave me massive confidence in the group, a belief that we could do well this season.

We had a good group here, but we were looking to add to it. Dan Ashworth told me that the club were keen to sign Ben Foster and he wanted

my opinion. I think it went something along the line of 'get him signed now', and fortunately we managed to do that one really early in the summer, which gave us that security, that piece of mind knowing that we had Ben tied up. He'd been the player of the year the previous season and it was really important to get him. If you're building a team, you have to build through the spine, and getting Ben at the back was important.

I was really keen to get a defensive midfield player and I spent the first three weeks going through a lot of DVDs. I think everyone will agree that we're quite fortunate that the one we whittled it down to was Claudio Yacob, who has turned out to be a fantastic signing for us. When you take someone from Argentina, they come halfway across the world, he didn't speak a word of English, my Spanish is not too hot either! It was difficult at the start for him, but once he was on the pitch he spoke a language that everybody could understand.

We brought in some firepower as well to score some goals. Romelu Lukaku is exciting and, from his little cameo against Liverpool on the opening day, that gave everybody a great feeling that we had this player that could come on and run at defenders and go past them as if they weren't there.

Liverpool was a good first game for us because I knew the expectation and the hype that surrounds Liverpool Football Club. Obviously, they had replaced Kenny Dalglish with Brendan Rodgers, and there was a feeling around Liverpool that it was going to be a great season, so they came here with high expectations where we'd just slipped under the radar a little bit. I knew approaching the first game that our preparation was spot on; I knew they were ready. We were hopeful of a good performance and with the good performance came a great win for us and that gave us the confidence to attack the early part of the season, which I think we did really well.

When Liverpool had good possession in the game, we didn't panic, we kept our shape well and we always looked a threat on the counter-attack and when the game opened up in the second half, especially after the red card, we were a big threat and we could have ended up with more than the three goals.

We'd taken confidence from beating Liverpool when we went down to White Hart Lane, which is always difficult. It was Tottenham's first home game of the season so obviously they were looking to put on a show for their new manager and it was a game where we didn't do much in the first half, but we showed enough to let Tottenham know that we could be a threat. Then they were fortunate to go ahead at a point where we were probably slightly the better team. They got a fortuitous goal off a deflection but from there, we really attacked the game, we went chasing it and we

got our reward, you know it was a late, late goal but it's one that you certainly couldn't begrudge us.

The win over Everton was the performance of the season for me. It was early in the season, we'd had the good home win to start, we'd had a difficult away fixture at Spurs and got ourselves a point, but I'd watched Everton play Manchester United in their first game of the season and I was really impressed, I thought they were a good team. I thought the game itself was evenly matched between two good sides and it changed a little bit on the substitutions. Everton made a couple of changes to try and go and win it, we matched them and fortunately for us it went in our favour. We got the first goal which allowed us to go on and get the second and for me it was almost a complete performance.

Then we let ourselves down at Fulham. After the long international break, the double headers when the players have been away for 12 days, most times, we struggled this season. Maybe I didn't freshen up the team enough after the international games. It's difficult for the players to go away, the travel and the pressure of playing for your country in vital qualifiers can obviously take its toll and we have to try and learn from it because no points from those three fixtures is a big hole in the season.

We didn't want the season to be a one week wonder, where you have three games at the start of the season and

everything's great but then suddenly it can go quickly wrong in the Premier League. Once you hit a run of average form, that's not enough in this league, you always have to be on top of your game. We spoke about it before the Reading game, the fact that the previous season, some of the so-called lesser teams in the division had come to The Hawthorns and got results, so we were determined not to let that happen again. We spoke about how it might not be the best footballing match, but the only important thing that day was to get the three points and that's what we managed to do.

It didn't quite work out at Villa unfortunately, we didn't take our chances. It was a good experience for me, my first derby here. Any derby game is really important

for the people involved, it's about pride and local bragging rights. I enjoyed the atmosphere, it was quite hostile, but I thought we played well that day. Obviously, going into the last 10 or 15 minutes and it's only one goal in front when maybe we should have had a couple, that makes it difficult. You know that any ball in the box can be dangerous and ultimately that's all it was, a ball in the box that fell to the wrong person at the wrong time and we only managed a 1-1.

This year we set out to try and make The Hawthorns a really difficult place for people to come. We had done that in the previous three matches, QPR were coming and they hadn't managed to get a win on the board so we knew they would be determined opponents. It was a game

a rugby pitch – I mean it's a very soft pitch and it can cut up a little bit so it's not always easy to play on. Although we'd put some really good performances in away from home, we hadn't actually won an away game, so it was nice to be able to show people that we could win away from home and it wasn't just going to be a season that relied solely on home performances, so that was a pleasing weekend.

Beating Chelsea? It's always nice to turn over your old club! When we go into games against any one of the top five or six clubs, you know that you have to be 100% concentrated on everything you do. I think we are a team where everyone has to play well and if that happens, especially at home, I think we are a match for anybody. We proved it that day against Chelsea.

After that, we went up to Sunderland in a great frame of mind, everything was going for us, when you are playing and winning all the time, you tend to get the little breaks that go in your favour. We went up there and we played some fantastic football and it was

We then lost a couple, so the Monday night game at home to Southampton was important. That was the night when winter started, it was freezing cold and then winter didn't go away after that but it was a good night, a good game. In spells they played well against us but we got in front and from there we controlled it quite well. Another clean sheet, and we got the second goal on a great counter-attack which had become a little bit of a trademark at that stage of the season.

A lot of teams don't like going to Wigan. For one it's

we went into with a lot of confidence and although the scoreline finished 3-2 – and I remember a horrific miss in the last minute from one of the QPR players – it was a game that we should have won much more comfortably.

another game where I don't think the final scoreline actually reflected the superiority we had that day.

After Sunderland, we were up to third, but certainly within our dressing room, we knew what we were trying to do, we knew where we were trying to go, we weren't carried away. It was great to be up there, it's always great to be successful, always good to win games, but that period was just a time for the supporters to pick up the papers and look at the league table and enjoy it. Unfortunately, we could only enjoy it for a couple of days because we had another really difficult midweek game. I think the fixture schedule was a little unkind to us. If we'd had a home game to follow the Sunderland game, I think this season might have been different. But from the North East we had to go all the way down to South Wales and it certainly wasn't our best performance of the season and we were well beaten at Swansea.

We slipped away a bit from there, in terms of results, not helped by some poor decisions at Arsenal. The penalty decisions changed the course of the game. Arsenal were not quite at their best and the longer the game was 0-0, the more chance we had to get something from it. But I think if we are being honest and we look back on the game, in the end Arsenal did enough to beat us on the day.

We managed the 0-0 at home to West Ham which stopped our run of defeats, which was important, you have to learn how to do that and then we

identified the Norwich game as one that we should win. I wasn't pleased with how we played the first half, it was around that time we were scratching around a little bit. We didn't start the game well, we went behind and from a losing position, we don't turn the game around very often. I thought the response of the players in the second half was good. Obviously we got the goal just before half-time which was key, it gave us that little bit of confidence to go chasing the game and we managed to turn a 1-0 deficit into a 2-1 victory which was a big win.

I think the Boxing Day game across London at the Arsenal had been called off because of the possible transport disruptions, but the FA and everyone else in their wisdom decided it was no problem for us to get past the busiest shopping centre in the world to get to Loftus Road to play

the game. It took us over an hour and a half to do a four mile journey. We got there just after two o'clock, fortunately QPR and the referee used their common sense and we kicked off a little bit late, but it didn't seem to affect us, we played well down there. We put in a really solid away performance and got what was a great three points.

I think if were being honest about it, the number of games you play in that Christmas and New Year spell did probably stretch us a little bit too far. If you lose three or four key players then it does affect the squad. We lost one or two key players around December and January and I think it showed, although we had players who were willing to go in and players who were going to give 100%. I could never criticise the effort or the application of the players who went in and tried to play in maybe

and you can keep it going but by the same token, if you go into a losing run you can also find it difficult to break that momentum. And that's what happened to us in January.

When you lose a late goal in a game, especially an FA Cup game, you know that can be fatal and unfortunately for us, it turned out that way. We lost the replay but the first game down there at Loftus Road, we should have won the game. When I came here I set a points target in the league and I also said that while you can't say that you're going to win a cup because obviously that's difficult, you can say that you want to treat them seriously. I think we did that in both competitions but it wasn't our year. I was disappointed to go out early but I can certainly promise the supporters that we don't take the cup competitions lightly and we want to try and have a good cup run next season.

After Christmas especially, we had some difficult games,

we'd played poorly at home to Fulham and lost, we went down to Reading and played well for 82 minutes and then switched off, and if you switch off, you get punished and that's what happened and I think the game at Reading took it out of us a little bit. We came into the Villa game knowing it was a big game for us. I think we put ourselves under a bit too much pressure, you could say in the first half that we didn't play at all so we went in lucky to be 2-0 down. We just had a calm chat with the players, saying that they had to play the second half for the supporters, they had to get back in the game, get the game to 2-1 and we knew that Villa, being down near the bottom of the league, would get nervous and that's how it turned out. Fortunately we managed to get the game back to 2-2 and, with a little bit of luck, I think we could have won it.

Chris Brunt scored a good goal for us and I

slightly different positions or positions that they are not quite comfortable with. It just seemed to take the edge off the season a little bit and in this league, it's easy to get into a little bit of a rut. It's good if you can get into a winning run

was pleased, because it was important for him at that time. Chris is the captain, he's maybe not someone everybody looks at and thinks he's an obvious captain but he is a leader, he leads by his character, the way he performs on the pitch. I think if I asked Chris to play in goal he'd say 'Ok, give me the gloves', he's that type of person. He wants to play for the team, he wants the team to do well and then his individual situation is secondary. He first and foremost wants the team

to be successful, and that's a fantastic trait to have.

We played well against Tottenham. Obviously the sending off of Goran Popov changed the complexion of the game but even against ten men, it took an unbelievable strike from Gareth Bale, who was in really hot form, to separate the two teams. I know Tottenham had a lot of the play in the second half and maybe we didn't threaten enough, but we stayed in the

game and at 1-0 we could have nicked something near the end but it started to show that from the second half against Villa, the season was starting to turn back in our favour again.

Winning at Anfield was a very important night for us. Liverpool were just starting to hit a bit of form, but I think the fact the players had been there the previous season and won, going to Anfield suddenly didn't seem to have the same fear about it.

We went down there, we played a good game, we started well, passed it well, looked a good team, although Liverpool got on top of us a bit in the second half. It took a really strange penalty decision from the referee to give them the chance to win it and, if I'm being honest, if they'd have scored the penalty they would probably have gone on to win it. But Ben Foster did what we know he can do and made a fantastic save from the penalty and from there it seemed to knock Liverpool out of their stride a little bit.

Last year when the Albion won 1-0, it was a lot more backs to the wall and there were a lot of chances that Liverpool actually created and missed whereas the game this year, although Liverpool had a lot of the ball and they had a lot of possession, the best chance and their only chance in the first half was when Steven Reid tried to chip it in his own net from under the crossbar and somehow he managed to put it over the crossbar which was an unbelievable clearance and another little sign that the season was starting to turn in our favour.

We'd reached a point in the season where we knew another couple of wins would see us safe and it was important to get there pretty much as early as we could. The Swansea game was a good game, we've been neck and neck with Swansea most of the season, they got what they deserved by winning the League Cup, they got great plaudits and everyone was speaking about Swansea, Swansea, Swansea and I used that as a little bit of motivation before the game to the players to say, "Look, all season we've been as good as, or better than Swansea, we've been in and around them all season, it's time for us to show the country that we're also a good team". I think the players took that on board and we won a really good match between two good teams. Then we backed it up by beating Sunderland.

I'm pleased we've had the chance to feature one or two younger players. It's important for any club to show the young players and to show the people that work in the academy and all the players that play in the academy that there is a path to the first team. If you don't show them that path, there's no point in having an academy, so it's really important. George Thorne came in at a point when we were struggling with injuries, we'd lost a few central midfield players. George had been at Peterborough and done very well, I'd been to see him a couple of times, and I was really pleased with his performances, I was getting great reports back so I thought the easiest thing to do was to bring him back and throw him into a game. It just happened to be

>

17

Manchester United at Old Trafford, but he was great on the day and it's a shame his season ended so abruptly with the injury at Goodison Park.

As a head coach for the first time, the hardest bit is when you work with the players all week and then you have to come to the final selection and sometimes you're leaving a really good player on the bench and sometimes it's even more difficult because you're leaving a really good player out of the squad altogether and you know the effort and the determination that they've shown through the week. When you name your team and your substitutes, you sometimes can see the disappointment, and that's probably the hardest part.

Everybody spoke about it being a great start, but the great start actually stretched all the way to December which becomes a little bit more

than a great start. The team showed in that first half of the season that they deserved to be up in the top six and I think for the supporters that was great, that they could see their team up there, challenging the big boys, standing toe to toe with them and it probably gave everybody that supports the Albion a great feeling

- it certainly gave us a great feeling in the dressing room.

We tailed off, you can't hide it, in the second half of the season it wasn't as good, it was more difficult, we lost our momentum, we lost our rhythm, and we lost some key players at key times. But I think you have to try and balance the season as a whole and I think for the club to be safe early in March and for us to enjoy the last few games without constantly having to scan the bottom three was probably an achievement in itself, it's a step forward for the club. ■

SEASON STATISTICS 2012-2013

DATE			OPPOSITION	SCORE	SCORERS
Sat	Aug	18	Liverpool	3-0	Gera, Odemwingie, Lukaku
Sat	Aug	25	Tottenham Hotspur	1-1	Morrison
Tue	Aug	28	Yeovil	4-2	Long 2, Brunt, Dawson
Sat	Sep	1	Everton	2-0	McAuley, Long
Sat	Sep	15	Fulham	0-3	
Sat	Sep	22	Reading	1-0	Lukaku
Wed	Sep	26	Liverpool	1-2	Tamas
Sun	Sep	30	Aston Villa	1-1	Long
Sat	Oct	6	Queens Park Rangers	3-2	Morrison, Gera, Mulumbu
Sat	Oct	20	Manchester City	1-2	Long
Sun	Oct	28	Newcastle United	1-2	Lukaku
Mon	Nov	5	Southampton	2-0	Odemwingie 2
Sat	Nov	10	Wigan Athletic	2-1	Morrison, og
Sat	Nov	17	Chelsea	2-1	Odemwingie, Long
Sat	Nov	24	Sunderland	4-2	Long, Gera, Lukaku, Fortune
Wed	Nov	28	Swansea City	1-3	Lukaku
Sat	Dec	1	Stoke City	0-1	
Sat	Dec	8	Arsenal	0-2	
Sun	Dec	16	West Ham United	0-0	
Sat	Dec	22	Norwich City	2-1	Gera, Lukaku
Wed	Dec	26	Queens Park Rangers	2-1	Brunt, og
Sat	Dec	29	Manchester United	0-2	
Tue	Jan	1	Fulham	1-2	Lukaku
Sat	Jan	5	Queens Park Rangers	1-1	Long
Sat	Jan	12	Reading	2-3	Lukaku 2
Wed	Jan	16	Queens Park Rangers	0-1	
Sat	Jan	19	Aston Villa	2-2	Brunt, Odemwingie
Wed	Jan	30	Everton	1-2	Long
Sun	Feb	3	Tottenham Hotspur	0-1	
Mon	Feb	11	Liverpool	2-0	McAuley, Lukaku
Sat	Feb	23	Sunderland	2-1	Lukaku 2
Sat	Mar	2	Chelsea	0-1	
Sat	Mar	9	Swansea City	2-1	Lukaku, og
Sat	Mar	16	Stoke City	0-0	
Sat	Mar	30	West Ham United	1-3	Dorrans
Sat	Apr	6	Arsenal	1-2	Morrison
Sat	Apr	20	Newcastle United	1-1	Jones
Sat	Apr	27	Southampton	3-0	Fortune, Long, Lukaku
Sat	May	4	Wigan Athletic	2-3	McAuley, Long
Tue	May	7	Manchester City	0-1	
Sun	May	12	Norwich City	0-4	
Sun	May	19	Manchester United	5-5	Lukaku 3, Morrison, Mulumbu

19

WHERE IN THE WORLD?

The Throstles have been all over the world during over 130 years of our history – have a look at this map of just a few of the places we've flown to, and the teams we have played there!

MAY 1959
Alberta All Star (Calgary, Canada)

JULY 1965
Ferencvaros (New York, USA)

NOV 1978
Valencia (Spain)

JULY 2011
San Jose Earthquakes (California, USA)

MAY 1965
Uruguay Select XI (Uruguay)

JULY 2012
Malmo
(Sweden)

NOV 1968
Dinamo
Bucharest
(Romania)

JUNE 1957
Dinamo
Tblisi
(USSR)

MARCH 1979
Red Star
Belgrade
(Yugoslavia)

MAY 1978
Shanghai
(China)

MAY 1978
Hong Kong
Select (Hong
Kong)

AUG 1978
Damascus
Police XI
(Syria)

MAY 1968
Uganda
National XI
(Uganda)

HUBERT PEARSON

ALBION APPEARANCES: **371**
ALBION GOALS: **2**
HONOURS WON WITH ALBION: **3**
(Championship 1920, FA Cup runner up 1912, promoted 1911)
INTERNATIONAL CAPS: **0**

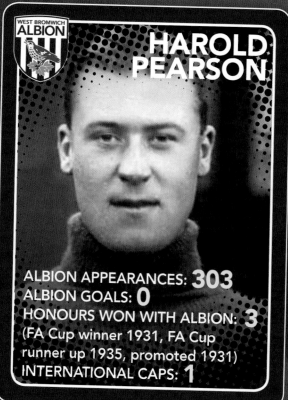

HAROLD PEARSON

ALBION APPEARANCES: **303**
ALBION GOALS: **0**
HONOURS WON WITH ALBION: **3**
(FA Cup winner 1931, FA Cup runner up 1935, promoted 1931)
INTERNATIONAL CAPS: **1**

PLAY YOUR ALBION CARDS RIGHT! GOALKEEPERS

There have been a number of great Albion teams over the years, but perhaps the best have been the 1920 League Champions, the 1931 double winners and the FA Cup winning teams of 1954 and 1968.

We've made some career cards for key players in all those teams and you'll find them throughout the pages of the annual, starting here with the goalkeepers. See who you think was the best – and how they compare with the players of today!

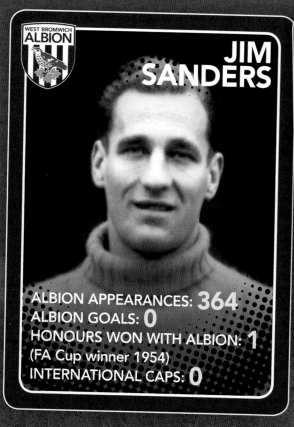

JIM SANDERS

ALBION APPEARANCES: **364**
ALBION GOALS: **0**
HONOURS WON WITH ALBION: **1**
(FA Cup winner 1954)
INTERNATIONAL CAPS: **0**

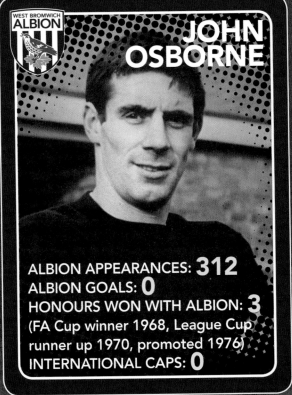

JOHN OSBORNE

ALBION APPEARANCES: **312**
ALBION GOALS: **0**
HONOURS WON WITH ALBION: **3**
(FA Cup winner 1968, League Cup runner up 1970, promoted 1976)
INTERNATIONAL CAPS: **0**

JUST SEVENTEEN!

Actually, Romelu Lukaku turned 20 during the course of last season, but the Chelsea loanee made a huge impression on the Albion faithful with a net busting 17 goals across the Premier League season – the most anybody has ever scored for us in a single season in that league.

From the moment he arrived on the scene as a sub against Liverpool on the opening day, outmuscling Jamie Carragher and then getting himself on the scoresheet, to the dying seconds of the finale with Manchester United when he masterminded the great escape as Albion recovered from three goals down to snatch an epic 5-5 draw, Lukaku was at the centre of Albion's season, scoring goals of every kind against all sorts of opposition.

It was a short-lived affair at The Hawthorns, but Romelu's contribution to establishing the Throstles in the top division means he will always have a place in Albion hearts! ■

23

BORN TO BE A BAGGIE

Tony Brown might have been born in Oldham and grown up a United fan in Manchester, but if ever anybody was born to be a Baggie, it's Bomber Brown!

28th September 2013, saw the 50th anniversary of his debut for the Albion – he scored, of course, in a 2-1 win away at Ipswich Town. It chalks up a half century of almost unbroken service to the cause, most notably as a brilliant goalscoring midfielder – one of the very best there's ever been – during which time he collected virtually every Albion record there was to get. Most league goals,

most club goals, most league appearances, most club appearances, those milestones belong to Tony Brown. He even went in goal a couple of times – and was never beaten!

He clocked up 720 games in all, scored a massive 279 goals, won the League Cup and FA Cup, was a League Cup runner-up twice, scored the goal that promoted us at Oldham in '76, played in

Europe and, more important than all of that, he's a brilliant bloke!

Still an Albion fan, he clocks up the miles criss-crossing the country to follow the Throstles as a commentator on Free Radio and a regular columnist in the Albion match programme. Make sure you get hold of a copy to see what's really going on with the beautiful game – Bomber knows! ■

LUGANO IS HERE!

Albion repeated last season's South American shopping spree that saw Argentina's Claudio Yacob come to The Hawthorns, but this season, we brought in a Uruguayan – their national captain, Diego Lugano!

Diego jumped at the chance to join Albion after receiving glowing references about the club from fellow countrymen Gus Poyet and Luis Suarez.

"I'm very glad to be here," said Lugano. "In fact, I'm thrilled. Playing in the English Premier League has always been my dream as I think it's the best league in the world.

Diego has captained Uruguay 77 times, more than any other player, and has also played in the Champions League and in top flight football across the world.

He is also the second highest capped player in his country's history, with only Diego Forlan having represented Uruguay more times – Diego won his 86th cap in Uruguay's Confederations Cup third/ fourth place play-off with Italy in Brazil in June.

The 32-year-old defender has also lifted the 2011 Copa America trophy – after beating Paraguay 3-0 in the final – and helped Uruguay reach the 2010 World Cup semi-finals.

Steve Clarke said, "I'm delighted to welcome Diego to the club. He's an experienced centre-half who will increase competition in that area of the team.

"Like some of the others we have here, Diego captains his country and is a leader. He has a real hunger and ambition to play and succeed in the Barclays Premier League and he will hopefully get a platform here to show everyone what he can do".

Lugano started his career in his native city with Club Atletico de Canelones. Shortly after turning 18, he joined the youth set-up at Montevideo giants Nacional.

He was involved in the side that won back-to-back championships in 2000 and 2001 but went on loan to Plaza Colonia in 2002, where he was made club captain.

Lugano joined Brazilian outfit Sao Paulo the following year, going on to win the FIFA Club World Championship and Copa Libertadores in 2005. The Brazilian 2006 Serie A title followed and he was voted the top defender in the country for the second successive season.

Later that year, he moved to Turkish side Fenerbahce where he spent five years and helped them win two Super Lig titles, two Turkish Super Cups, one Turkish Cup and also reach the 2007/08 Champions League quarter-finals before moving to Paris Saint-Germain in August 2011. Injury limited him to 12 appearances for them before he joined Malaga on loan in 2012.

"I chose Albion because it is a club that is developing a lot. They had a very good season last season and I hope to help the team repeat that or even improve on it.

"I have some very good friends working and playing in this country and I asked them about Albion. What did they say? Well, Suarez told me Liverpool got beaten twice by Albion last season, so that was a very good reference!

"Both he and Poyet said Albion play very good football and are a serious club which wants to accomplish something – and my first impression of the club is amazing.

"The references I got about Albion were just the best. Being in England and playing in the Premier League is just amazing for me. I'm very, very happy.

"I pride myself in being professional. I try to bring a good energy into the changing room – regardless of results. It's important to stay positive, whether you're winning or losing". ■

HAT-TRICK HEROES!

When Romelu Lukaku helped himself to a hat-trick on the last day of last season against Manchester United to earn that unbelievable 5-5 draw, he became only the fourth Albion man to get to keep the matchball for his goalscoring exploits in Premier League history.

The last day of the season has a habit of producing Albion heroes because back in May 2011, we were trailing 3-0 at Newcastle United before super Somen Tchoyi stepped up to score three second half goals to make sure we left Tyneside with a 3-3 draw.

Our first Premier League hat-trick couldn't have been more important. It came in March 2005 as the Throstles headed for south London and a tough game at Charlton. Deep in relegation trouble, defeat could have been disastrous but after Robert Earnshaw's hat-trick, we came away 4-1 winners and on the way to the "Great Escape"!

Maybe the most memorable of them all came in February 2012 though, just down the road at Molineux. As Albion took Wolves apart, Peter Odemwingie was on hand to help himself to three goals as the Baggies won 5-1, setting ourselves up for a top half finish and sending the Wolves on the way down.

PLAY YOUR ALBION CARDS RIGHT!
DEFENDERS

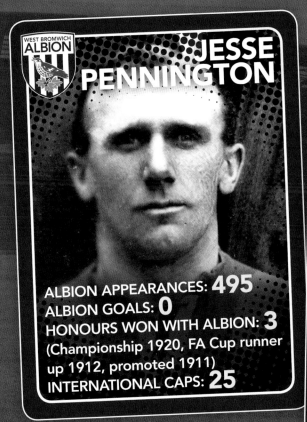

JESSE PENNINGTON

ALBION APPEARANCES: **495**
ALBION GOALS: **0**
HONOURS WON WITH ALBION: **3**
(Championship 1920, FA Cup runner up 1912, promoted 1911)
INTERNATIONAL CAPS: **25**

GEORGE SHAW

ALBION APPEARANCES: **425**
ALBION GOALS: **11**
HONOURS WON WITH ALBION: **3**
(FA Cup winner 1931, FA Cup runner up 1935, promoted 1931)
INTERNATIONAL CAPS: **1**

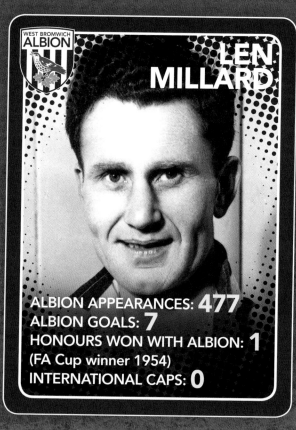

LEN MILLARD

ALBION APPEARANCES: **477**
ALBION GOALS: **7**
HONOURS WON WITH ALBION: **1**
(FA Cup winner 1954)
INTERNATIONAL CAPS: **0**

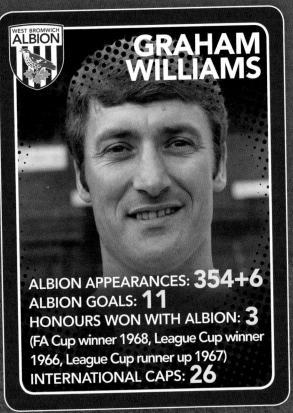

GRAHAM WILLIAMS

ALBION APPEARANCES: **354+6**
ALBION GOALS: **11**
HONOURS WON WITH ALBION: **3**
(FA Cup winner 1968, League Cup winner 1966, League Cup runner up 1967)
INTERNATIONAL CAPS: **26**

SPOT THE BALL

When Jonas Olsson goes up for a header, everybody on the opposition team gets nervous – including the ball!

The ball got so frightened this time that it disappeared altogether – where do you think it should be?

Answer on page 61.

GOAL OF
THE SEASON!

Zoltan Gera helped himself to the "Goal of the Season" award last term – and he didn't waste much time doing it, did he? His winning strike came in the first half of the first game of the campaign, a smashing volley that flew in beyond Pepe Reina and into the top corner of the Smethwick End goal.

It was a real screamer from the popular Hungarian and perhaps the closest challenger to that brilliant season starter came from Zoltan himself, another long range screamer up at Sunderland's Stadium of Light.

Back to fitness after having his season ended early by injury at Loftus Road in January, you can be certain that Zoltan will be looking to carry off the award again this season! ■

UNMI55ABLE!

The Premier League had never seen anything like it. Sir Alex Ferguson, in his 1,500th and final game in charge of Manchester United hadn't had a day to match it. Even The Hawthorns, 113 years old, hadn't experienced anything to match up to this.

With the ground packed to the absolute rafters to witness the final day of Sir Alex's career, they were treated to a typically swaggering start from the 20-time champions, United racing off into a 3-0 lead in the first half an hour. They were so much in control that even when James Morrison clipped in a goal before the break, few thought it would make much difference.

The arrival of Romelu Lukaku at the break changed everything though. He dragged it back to 3-2 with a sweet finish before United found their feet again and extended the lead to 5-2, a lead they kept up to the 80th minute.

And then it all went a bit crazy!

With two goals inside a minute, Lukaku and Youssouf Mulumbu had brought the score back to 5-4 and with five minutes left to play, Romelu equalised, completing a perfect hat-trick by heading in while on his hands and knees!

The game ended 5-5, the first ever result like that in Premier League history. No wonder both sets of fans spent ages celebrating after the final whistle! ■

SIR ALEX FERGUSON

DESIGN OUR KIT!

No wonder Billy Jones is looking worried as he looks down at his Albion shirt – somebody has stolen the colours!

Can you design a new home or away shirt for the Throstles to cheer Billy up again?!?

PLAY YOUR ALBION CARDS RIGHT!
MIDFIELDERS

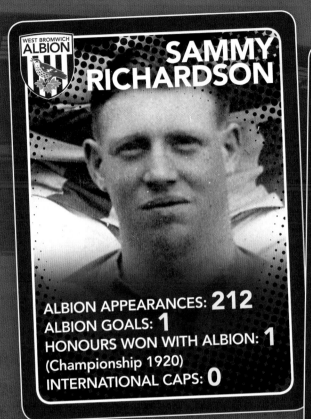

SAMMY RICHARDSON

ALBION APPEARANCES: **212**
ALBION GOALS: **1**
HONOURS WON WITH ALBION: **1**
(Championship 1920)
INTERNATIONAL CAPS: **0**

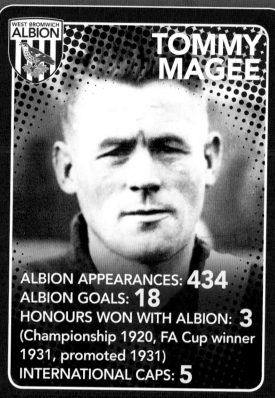

TOMMY MAGEE

ALBION APPEARANCES: **434**
ALBION GOALS: **18**
HONOURS WON WITH ALBION: **3**
(Championship 1920, FA Cup winner 1931, promoted 1931)
INTERNATIONAL CAPS: **5**

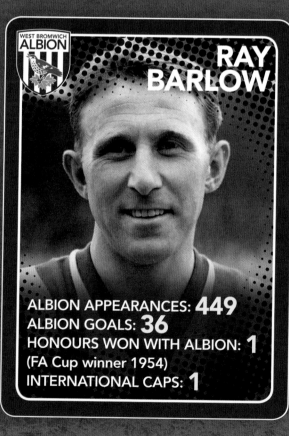

RAY BARLOW

ALBION APPEARANCES: **449**
ALBION GOALS: **36**
HONOURS WON WITH ALBION: **1**
(FA Cup winner 1954)
INTERNATIONAL CAPS: **1**

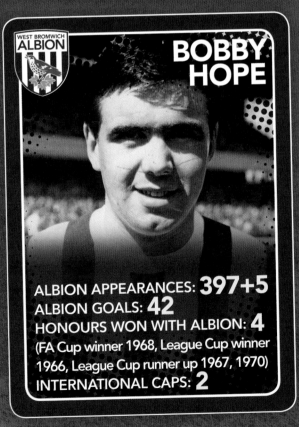

BOBBY HOPE

ALBION APPEARANCES: **397+5**
ALBION GOALS: **42**
HONOURS WON WITH ALBION: **4**
(FA Cup winner 1968, League Cup winner 1966, League Cup runner up 1967, 1970)
INTERNATIONAL CAPS: **2**

THE BIG QUIZ

How well do you know your history? We've got some Albion questions about each season from 1999/2000 to 2012/13 – see how much you know about your favourites!

Answers on page 61.

1. Gary Megson joined as Albion manager in early 2000. Who did he replace?

2. We had to win our last game of the 1999/2000 season to stay up – who did we beat?

3. Albion reached the promotion play-offs in May 2001. Who did we play?

4. The East Stand was opened at the start of the 2001/02 season. Who were our first opponents at home that season?

5. We won at Bradford in April 2002 to set up a final day promotion party – who scored the vital penalty there?

6. Who scored Albion's first ever Premier League goal in August 2002?

7. Albion signed a Nigerian international from Arsenal in the summer of 2004. Who?

8. Gary Megson left Albion in October 2004. Who was his last game against?

9. Albion achieved "the Great Escape" on the last day of the 2004/05 season – who did we beat to stay up?

10. Which player became the first to score 10 goals in a Premier League season for Albion in 2004/05?

11. Which striker did Albion sign from Aston Villa in August 2006?

12. Tony Mowbray replaced who as Albion manager in October 2006?

13. Who beat Albion in the play-off final at Wembley in May 2007?

14. Name one of two ex-Albion men in the opposition that day?

15. Who scored Albion's goal in the 1-1 draw with Southampton that guaranteed promotion in April 2008?

16. Who became Albion's record signing in the summer of 2008?

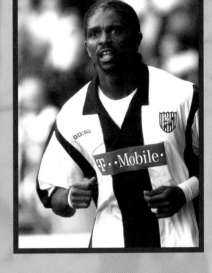

17. Which club did Tony Mowbray leave Albion to join in the summer of 2009?

18. Who replaced him as head coach?

19. Who did Albion beat to clinch promotion in April 2010?

20. Who was the top scorer in that promotion winning season of 2009/10?

21. Who were Roy Hodgson's first opponents as Albion's head coach in 2011?

22. Who scored a hat-trick on the final day of the 2010/11 season?

23. Which former Wolves player scored for us in our 5-1 win at Molineux in February 2012?

24. Who won the player of the season award for 2011/12?

25. How many goals did Romelu Lukaku score in 2012/13?

26. And how many points did Albion get in that season?

If you're lucky, you'll have sat and watched the Albion at The Hawthorns, but did you know that wasn't our original home ground?

Like most clubs, Albion's early days saw them wandering around looking for somewhere to play. We started off back in the late 1870s by playing on a patch of ground between Walsall Street and Beeches Road, before moving to the rather posher surroundings of Dartmouth Park.

THE SHINING CITY on the HILL

But as the club grew in stature, rapidly becoming a force in the area, we needed a more permanent home, one that was enclosed so that admission could be charged. It was back to the beginning, back to Walsall Street and a site called Bunn's Field, the club's players and officials putting up the fencing ahead of the 1881/82 season.

Yet within a year, we had outgrown it and moved instead to the Four Acres, home of Dartmouth Cricket Club, sharing the ground with them. We played our first game in the FA Cup there, defeat at home to Wednesbury Old Athletic on 10th November 1883. The following season, we went as far as round six before losing to Blackburn Rovers in front of 16,393, the Four Acres

becoming a victim of its own success as we again needed bigger premises.

We cast our seeds upon stony ground, or, more accurately, Stoney Lane, the site that was to host a spell of extraordinary success for the Throstles and give us that nickname. The team changed in the Plough & Harrow pub next to the ground, the pub's landlady keeping a throstle in a cage. As they left for the game, if the throstle was singing, that was taken as a good omen for the game. When we looked for a club crest in 1895, a throstle was the obvious choice.

Stoney Lane was opened on 5 September 1885, with a visit from Glasgow's Third Lanark Rifle Volunteers. Albion won 5-0, setting us on the pathway to becoming one of the

biggest clubs in the country.

The luck of the draw gave us five home ties in the 1885/86 FA Cup as we made it all the way to the final, only to lose to Blackburn Rovers in a replay, and we were beaten in the following year's final by Villa. A hat-trick of final appearances was completed in 1888 when, against all the odds, we defeated Preston North End, then the biggest spending and most feared club in the country.

There was another cup final win in 1892, 3-0 against the Villa, and a defeat against the same opposition at the same stage in 1895, but while the Throstles could pack them in for cup games, the figures for league fixtures remained low, down in four figures more often than not. As the lease came close to expiring on Stoney Lane, the club needed to find a bigger home.

So it was that in May 1900, we set footballing precedent once again by creating the first out of town football ground. ∎

THE HAWTHORNS

We didn't have **floodlights** at the ground until 1957. Before then, all games had to be played in daylight – even in midweek!

We played our first game at The Hawthorns on 3rd September 1900, and drew 1-1 with Derby County. The first goal was scored by Derby's England forward Steve Bloomer, and Chippy Simmons equalised for Albion.

England have played three senior internationals at The Hawthorns, against Ireland, Belgium and Wales. England's women also played their Italian counterparts in 1998.

The **current capacity** of the stadium is 26,586.

The Hawthorns became an **all-seater stadium** in 1995 and was officially opened as such on Boxing Day 1995 when we beat Bristol City 1-0.

The **record attendance** at The Hawthorns came against Arsenal in the sixth round of the FA Cup on 6th March 1937, when 64,815 crammed into the ground.

The Hawthorns is the **highest** league ground in England, at **551 feet above sea level.**

The **big TV screens** were installed at either end of the ground in time for the start of the Premier League season of 2002/03.

We won the League Cup at The Hawthorns in 1966. It was a two legged final in those days and having lost the first game 2-1 at West Ham, we won the return 4-1. Not bad against Bobby Moore, Geoff Hurst and Martin Peters!

Football isn't the only game that's been played there – we've seen cricket, athletics meetings and even baseball!

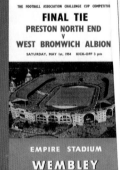

The 1954 FA Cup winners. Albion parade the trophy around Wembley after their victory over Preston.

The current Albion team is doing pretty well for itself, isn't it? But even they can't match the exploits of the team from 60 years ago, the team of 1953/54 who very nearly did the first league and cup double of the 20th century.

The team led by manager Vic Buckingham had been pretty impressive the previous season, but they opened up 1953/54 in awesome form. Albion won 12 of our first 15 games that season, losing only once. We won 7-3 away at

Newcastle and 4-1 at Burnley inside four days, beat Chelsea 5-2 and scored goals as if it were the easiest thing in the world.

With Ronnie Allen and Johnnie Nicholls in great goalscoring form and the great Ray Barlow the kind of midfield playmaker that would cost you £30 million these days, Albion were a treat to watch, playing a new, more cultured kind of game.

After Christmas, we had to battle it out on two fronts,

as we looked to collect both trophies in the same season. We beat Chelsea and Rotherham United in the early rounds before having another epic battle with Newcastle United in round five. This was at The Hawthorns and a Ronnie Allen hat-trick saw us to a 3-2 victory.

We beat Tottenham in round six and our reward was a tie with Third Division Port Vale at Villa Park in the semi-final. We went behind but finally scraped through 2-1 winners.

THE CENTURY

We were still in the running for the league title at that point, but we suffered a terrible injury crisis that knocked us off-balance. We also saw Allen and Nicholls called up to play for England on the same day that we were playing our main rivals for the title, Wolves. Under strength, and seeing Barlow injured in the first few minutes, Albion were beaten 1-0 and the league slipped away from us.

But there was still the FA Cup Final and a meeting with Preston at Wembley in front of 99,852 fans. Albion took an early lead through Allen, but then Preston came back at us, going 2-1 ahead. As the minutes slipped away, Barlow raced into the box and was fouled. Penalty! Up stepped Ronnie Allen to score the crucial kick.

Extra-time looked certain but with a few minutes to go, winger Frank Griffin burst into the box and won the game with a low shot.

So good were Albion that season that one newspaper called them the "Team of the Century" and suggested that they should be sent to represent England in the 1954 World Cup that summer. Pity that Paddy Ryan was Irish and Jimmy Dudley was a Scot! ■

SOUTH GRAND STAND

ENTER AT TURNSTILES
(See Plan and Conditions on back)

ENTRANCE K 42

Row 23   Seat 3

Empire Stadium, Wembley

THE FOOTBALL ASSOCIATION CUP COMPETITION

FINAL TIE

SATURDAY, MAY 1st, 1954
Kick-off 3 p.m.

Price 25/-
(Including Tax)

CHAIRMAN AND MANAGING DIRECTOR
Wembley Stadium Limited.

THIS PORTION TO BE RETAINED
This Ticket is issued on the condition that it is not re-sold for more than its face value.

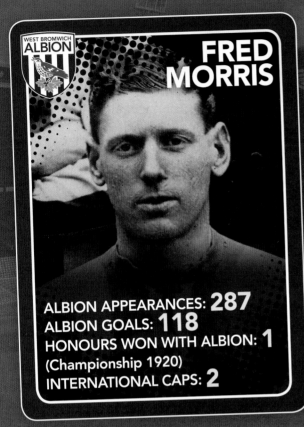

FRED MORRIS

ALBION APPEARANCES: **287**
ALBION GOALS: **118**
HONOURS WON WITH ALBION: **1**
(Championship 1920)
INTERNATIONAL CAPS: **2**

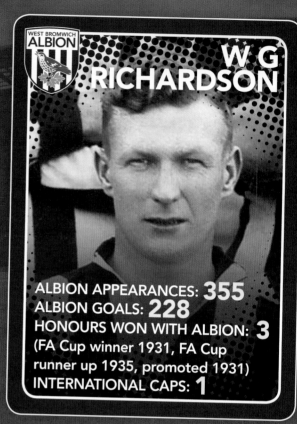

W G RICHARDSON

ALBION APPEARANCES: **355**
ALBION GOALS: **228**
HONOURS WON WITH ALBION: **3**
(FA Cup winner 1931, FA Cup
runner up 1935, promoted 1931)
INTERNATIONAL CAPS: **1**

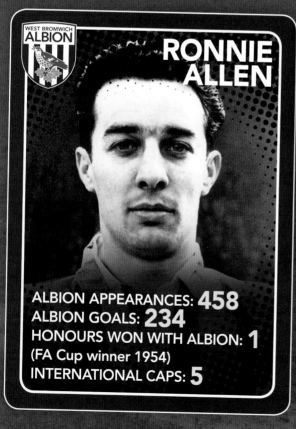

RONNIE ALLEN

ALBION APPEARANCES: **458**
ALBION GOALS: **234**
HONOURS WON WITH ALBION: **1**
(FA Cup winner 1954)
INTERNATIONAL CAPS: **5**

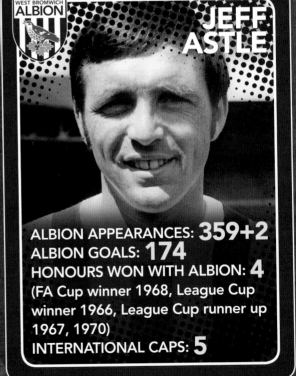

JEFF ASTLE

ALBION APPEARANCES: **359+2**
ALBION GOALS: **174**
HONOURS WON WITH ALBION: **4**
(FA Cup winner 1968, League Cup
winner 1966, League Cup runner up
1967, 1970)
INTERNATIONAL CAPS: **5**

WORDSEARCH

We've got the diggers in to help us search for these Albion words at the training ground! Can you help find them? Answers on page 61.

ALBION   **CLARKE**   **MULUMBU**
ANELKA   **JONAS**   **TONY BROWN**
BILLY   **MCAULEY**   **WBA**

```
T  G  W  X  M  I  A  W  B  A  M
O  D  B  I  L  L  Y  C  B  V  U
N  A  A  L  H  O  F  B  S  S  L
Y  O  F  I  F  Z  F  O  M  F  U
B  R  A  E  O  L  C  Q  C  P  M
R  R  Z  A  N  E  L  K  A  U  B
O  S  M  L  B  D  A  F  U  L  U
W  J  O  B  R  G  R  H  L  Y  P
N  U  S  I  L  D  K  O  E  J  R
R  L  Y  O  O  W  E  X  Y  Z  H
F  J  O  N  A  S  L  A  R  I  E
```

Albion winger Scott Sinclair admitted that fan power helped persuade him to sign for the club after his Twitter account was bombarded by supporters desperate to get him to sign for us!

TWEETS for a THROSTLE!

"The Albion fans have been on Twitter telling me how great it would be for me to come down," said Sinclair. "I'm looking forward to repaying them by scoring some goals.

"I'm very happy to be an Albion player and I'm looking forward to this season. I can't wait to get some games under my belt."

The former Manchester City man made six loan moves in as many years, but hopes he is now able to settle down at The Hawthorns.

"I've been on loan a few times, which has been annoying sometimes," added Sinclair. "When I was younger, it was to get experience. But this time I'm not coming out for experience, I'm coming out to play games. I want to settle down and stop going from loan to loan.

"I like the style of football Albion play and that's why I chose to come here and play for Steve Clarke. I know him previously from my Chelsea days and I'm excited to be playing for him again.

"I sat down with my family and Steve Clarke being at West Brom helped us make the decision when we were discussing where the best place for me to come was at this point of my career.

"I've spoken to Steve throughout, we know each other well, and there isn't a better place for me to come than here. Albion play good football and it's great for me to come into this side."

"Scott understands he needs to play football and it will be good to work with him again," said Clarke.

"We're delighted he feels this is the right club for him at this stage of his career. He is the type of player we were missing from the squad.

"He is a pure winger, who is quick, direct and scores goals – he has proven that over his career. He can play off the right or left and improves our attacking options.

"I know him well and he is a good person, who I know is 100 percent committed to our cause. He is frustrated that

44

he did not get the chances to play at Manchester City last season and, hopefully, he will take those frustrations out on Premier League defenders this season."

The Bath-born forward joined Bristol Rovers as a nine-year-old and became their second-youngest debutant – aged 15 years and 277 days – in a League Two clash with Leyton Orient in December 2004.

Chelsea snapped him up for a tribunal-set fee in July 2005 and he spent five years with the London club. He made his first-team debut as a late substitute in a League Cup semi-final clash with Wycombe Wanderers in January 2007.

Sinclair, who scored his first senior goal for Chelsea in a 4-0 League Cup win over Hull during the 2007/08 campaign, enjoyed loan spells at Plymouth, QPR, Charlton and Crystal Palace to gain first-team experience.

The 5ft 8in ace also spent the second half of the 2008/09 season at Birmingham, helping them win automatic promotion to the top flight. Sinclair's form encouraged Wigan to snap him up for the following campaign, when he made his first real impact on the Barclays Premier League under then-Latics boss Roberto Martinez.

In summer 2010, he joined Swansea on a permanent basis and quickly became a fans' favourite at the Liberty Stadium. He scored 19 goals in his first season for the Swans, including a play-off final hat-trick in a 4-2 Wembley win over Reading to make them the first Welsh club to reach the Barclays Premier League.

Sinclair carried that form into the top flight, scoring eight goals in 37 games, prompting then-Premier League champions City to splash £6.2 million to take him to the Etihad Stadium. ∎

PLAYER OF THE SEASON: GARETH McAULEY

Gareth McAuley turned out to be the star turn of an epic 2012/13 Albion season. He walked off with the Albion Oscars for Players' Player of the Year and Supporters' Player of the Year, a pretty decent haul for the Northern Irish international. This is what he had to say straight after picking up the gongs...

"To win the vote for Player of the Year from the players and from the supporters is about as good as it gets and I was just buzzing to pick up both prizes.

"Coming into the Premier League so late, there are always doubts about whether you can play there from other people, so I'm very proud that the people in the stands and the guys in the dressing room have recognised that I can do a job in the top division.

"I can only thank Roy Hodgson for giving me that chance in the first place, Steve Clarke for carrying on putting me in the team, and all the coaches and the players here who work with me every day and who have helped me to make a contribution. For the gaffer, in his first season in charge he has done a great job, it's been such an easy transition for us to work for him after Roy. He makes us work hard, training is enjoyable but tough, and that is important. He has the personal touch as well which maybe people on the outside don't see, but he is very good with all the players and we do enjoy working for him.

"It's been a long road, even after I joined the Albion. I came in for preseason and straight away I was struggling with a virus, I lost all my strength, my power, everything, and I was actually quite worried about it for a while. In the end, I actually had to admit defeat on that one, stop trying to work through it and instead take a step back, just go away and rest for a while. That was when I started on the road to recovery, got my strength back and when I got my chance in the team in a cup game up at Everton, I was determined to take it. Since then, I've been fortunate with injuries.

"The important thing is to be consistent, not just play really well for a couple of games and then drop off from that standard. My aim is just to play football matches, to be the best I can be every time I go out on the field. All of us have an off day now and again but as long as I come off the pitch knowing that I tried my best for my team mates, then you can't do more than that. This is a fantastic place to play football, I love being with the lads, there's a good atmosphere here, and I hope I can be a part of that for a good while yet.

"It's always good to play alongside Jonas. We've built up a great partnership over the last couple of seasons and so hopefully that will continue for a few more years to come yet. And the two of us benefit from having Claudio and Youssouf in front of us. Claudio was a bit of an unknown quantity when he arrived, but we knew from day one in preseason that he was going to be some player for us. First training session he had, you could see he loved a tackle, he got stuck right in and left it on a few boys so I thought from there that he would do for us! He's a good lad, a real worker, great playing in that position in front of us, and he's the one I voted for as player of the year.

"Maybe I should have my eye set on winning goal of the season next year to complete the set? Not enough headers get into the running for that, so maybe we ought to change that – I'd like to win it just to put the cat among the pigeons with the strikers!" ∎

OUR MATE MATEJ!

Albion are looking for goals in 2013/14 – after signing Nicolas Anelka, in came young Matej Vydra in time for the big kick off.

The 21-year-old Czech striker joined the Throstles on a season-long loan from Udinese and is relishing the chance to work under Steve Clarke in the Barclays Premier League.

After firing 22 Championship goals for Watford in 2012/13, he is also chomping at the bit to link up with fellow summer signing Nicolas Anelka.

And, after speaking to Clarke's former Chelsea teammate and current Hornets manager Gianfranco Zola for advice, he is delighted to have secured a Hawthorns move.

"I didn't know if I was coming back to England this season, but I am very pleased to become a West Bromwich Albion player and I will do my best for the team," said Vydra.

"There was a lot of club interest from around Europe and England, but I choose West Bromwich Albion because of the head coach.

"He is one of the best managers in England and plays a European style.

"I spoke briefly to my former coach Zola on the telephone and he advised me to go to West Bromwich Albion because the style of play will suit me.

"I think it is a good choice for me.

"Another reason I chose West Bromwich Albion is because it is a great opportunity to play alongside a big striker like Nicolas Anelka.

"I had a very good season last year and I would like to continue that form.

"Of course I can't promise how many goals I will score but the most important thing is the club.

"I'm very quick, I think I'm dangerous in the penalty area, and I can shoot with my left or right foot.

"I want to play each game and do everything I can to help my teammates win games." ■

WHOSE BOOTS?

Gone are the days when footballers used to wear plain black boots – ask your dad!

Nowadays, Albion's finest come kitted out in the flashiest footwear, but just whose feet are in these boots?

Answers on page 61.

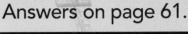

PLAYER PROFILES

BEN FOSTER

Birthdate: 3 April 1983
Position: Goalkeeper
Height: 1.93m
Weight: 90kg
Other clubs: Stafford Rangers, Stoke City, Manchester United, Birmingham City
Albion games: 70
Albion goals: 0

Ben's second season with the Throstles was every bit as good as his first, the former Manchester United and Birmingham City goalkeeper crowning another fine campaign by returning to the England squad under Roy Hodgson towards the end of the season. His finest moment of last season probably came in the 2-0 win at Anfield where a string of brilliant saves included keeping out a penalty from Steven Gerrard in front of the Kop.

BOAZ MYHILL

Birthdate: 9 November 1982
Position: Goalkeeper
Height: 1.91m
Weight: 92kg
Other clubs: Aston Villa, Hull City
Albion games: 22
Albion goals: 0

Boaz Myhill returned to The Hawthorns last season after a yearlong loan spell at Birmingham City, where he played in the Europa League, and immediately started to try to put pressure on Albion's number one, Ben Foster. He got his chance through injury to Foster in November and played in seven games in a row as Albion briefly moved into the Champions League places. The Welsh international also featured in the FA Cup against QPR.

STEVEN REID

Birthdate: 10 March 1981
Position: Right-back
Height: 1.85m
Weight: 87kg
Other clubs: Millwall, Blackburn Rovers
Albion games: 59+12
Albion goals: 4

Steven Reid continued his stay at The Hawthorns by signing a new one year contract in the summer of 2013. Last season was a frustrating one for him after a number of niggling injuries stopped him from getting a run of games in the team at any stage. Since joining from Blackburn, initially on loan towards the end of the 2009/10 season, his experience has played a big part in helping Albion re-establish ourselves as a Premier League force.

PLAYER PROFILES

BILLY JONES

Birthdate: 24 March 1987
Position: Right-back
Height: 1.82m
Weight: 79kg
Other clubs: Crewe Alexandra, Preston North End
Albion games: 48+4
Albion goals: 1

In his second season at The Hawthorns, Billy Jones really began to establish himself as a regular in the side, with a string of accomplished performances at right-back that included plenty of attacking runs down the right that contributed to Albion goals, Billy scoring his first for the club at The Hawthorns in the 1-1 draw with Newcastle United. Building on last season's success is his priority for the 2013/14 campaign.

LIAM RIDGEWELL

Birthdate: 21 July 1984
Position: Left-back
Height: 1.88m
Weight: 78kg
Other clubs: West Ham United, Bournemouth, Aston Villa, Birmingham City
Albion games: 43+2
Albion goals: 1

Liam Ridgewell completed his first full season with the Albion by winning his battle for the left-back spot against Goran Popov. Liam was a regular for most of the season, though he was unable to add to the single goal he has managed thus far for the club. Having played for both Birmingham City and Aston Villa, he made his escape out of the second city and into the Black Country in the transfer window of January 2012.

JONAS OLSSON

Birthdate: 10 March 1983
Position: Centre-half
Height: 1.93m
Weight: 84kg
Other clubs: Landskrona, NEC Nijmegen
Albion games: 172+1
Albion goals: 11

Jonas Olsson clocked up yet another influential season for the Albion as we finished eighth in 2012/13, his fifth season at The Hawthorns during which time he has been among our most consistent players. His partnership with Gareth McAuley was one of the foundations of our success, though Jonas was not as prolific at the other end of the pitch as his colleague, failing to add to his 11 previous Albion goals.

GARETH McAULEY

Birthdate: 5 December 1979
Position: Centre-half
Height: 1.95m
Weight: 90kg
Other clubs: Coleraine, Lincoln City, Leicester City, Ipswich Town
Albion games: 73+1
Albion goals: 5

The 2012/13 season was a personal triumph for Gareth McAuley who picked up the Player of the Year trophy from both the supporters and his fellow players. The Northern Irish international was a late starter in professional football, and later still in the Premier League, but he's more than made up for lost time over the last couple of seasons, earning himself a new deal to extend his stay at The Hawthorns.

PLAYER PROFILES

CRAIG DAWSON

Birthdate: 6 May 1990
Position: Centre-half
Height: 1.88m
Weight: 85kg
Other clubs: Rochdale
Albion games: 11+5
Albion goals: 0

Craig Dawson might not have added too many games to his Albion tally last season, but he had a very busy year nonetheless, starting with representing Great Britain in the 2012 Olympics and ending up as a member of England's Under 21 team at the European Championships in Israel, scoring his side's only goal of the competition. A lengthy loan spell at Bolton Wanderers also saw him help the Trotters to the verge of promotion to the Premier League.

PLAYER PROFILES

GABRIEL TAMAS

Birthdate: 9 November 1983
Position: Centre-half
Height: 1.88m
Weight: 79kg
Other clubs: Dinamo Bucharest, Celta Vigo, Auxerre, Galatasaray
Albion games: 66+11
Albion goals: 3

Romanian international Gabriel Tamas played an important part in Albion's success last season, deputising on occasion for both Gareth McAuley and Jonas Olsson and living up to the standards that those two set. Gabriel is a bit of an Albion veteran now, having joined us in January 2010, becoming a very important member of the team that won promotion under Roberto Di Matteo that season.

CLAUDIO YACOB

Birthdate: 18 July 1987
Position: Central midfielder
Height: 1.81m
Weight: 73kg
Other clubs: Racing Club de Avellaneda
Albion games: 29+1
Albion goals: 0

Claudio Yacob was a major signing for the club last summer when he came to England from Argentina and slotted straight into the Albion side as a holding midfielder, playing as if he had been in this country all his life. An injury just before Christmas disrupted his season but he returned to the team and resumed his excellent partnership with Youssouf Mulumbu. Yacob's ability to spot danger and then to stop it quickly was a huge part of Albion's defensive strength last term.

CHRIS BRUNT

Birthdate: 14 December 1984
Position: Winger
Height: 1.87m
Weight: 85kg
Other clubs: Sheffield Wednesday
Albion games: 184+36
Albion goals: 36

The Albion captain had a few injury problems at the start of last season, but once they cleared up he played a big role in the team, either from his preferred position out on the wing or filling in from a more central role when the likes of Mulumbu or Yacob were missing. The ultimate team player, Chris' corners proved to be one of our most dangerous attacking weapons across the season, plenty of Albion goals coming from his set pieces.

GRAHAM DORRANS

Birthdate: 5 May 1987
Position: Midfielder
Height: 1.79m
Weight: 78kg
Other clubs: Livingston
Albion games: 117+33
Albion goals: 23

Scottish international Graham Dorrans struggled to find a place in the Albion team in the first half of last season, but after the turn of the year he became a regular in the midfield once again, playing out wide or more centrally. He clocked up his 150th Albion appearance during the season and added one more goal to his tally for the club, scoring from the penalty spot in the 3-1 defeat at West Ham United.

PLAYER PROFILES

YOUSSOUF MULUMBU

Birthdate: 25 January 1987
Position: Central midfielder
Height: 1.74m
Weight: 76kg
Other clubs: Paris St Germain
Albion games: 138+14
Albion goals: 13

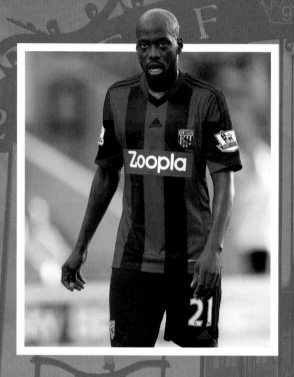

Youssouf Mulumbu produced another inspirational season for the Albion, in spite of being away from The Hawthorns for a month as he represented DR Congo in the African Cup of Nations. Youssouf has now played over 150 games for the Throstles since joining us in January 2009 and he has now taken his goalscoring record to 13, the 13th being lucky for us as it was the fourth goal in our stunning comeback against Manchester on the last day of last season!

JAMES MORRISON

Birthdate: 25 May 1986
Position: Central midfielder
Height: 1.80m
Weight: 75kg
Other clubs: Middlesbrough
Albion games: 153+34
Albion goals: 23

James ended his season on a high, not just by scoring against Manchester United again, but also by captaining Scotland in an international. Morrison was a very influential member of Albion's side, especially when we adopted the lone striker formation, James playing in behind Shane Long or Romelu Lukaku and both scoring and creating plenty of goals for the Albion. He'll be looking forward to breaking through the 200 appearances mark for the club in 2013/14.

ZOLTAN GERA

Birthdate: 22 April 1979
Position: Midfielder
Height: 1.83m
Weight: 75kg
Other clubs: Ferencvaros, Fulham
Albion games: 135+41
Albion goals: 29

For the second year running, Zoltan Gera found his season disrupted by injury, though this time around, he had time to register Albion's "Goal of the Season", his stunning volley against Liverpool on the opening day setting Albion up for a highly successful campaign. If that wasn't enough to get people going, the popular Hungarian midfielder's strike at Sunderland's Stadium of Light in our 4-2 win was pretty special as well!

PLAYER PROFILES

GEORGE THORNE

Birthdate: 4 January 1993
Position: Central midfielder
Height: 1.88m
Weight: 84kg
Albion games: 11+6
Albion goals: 0

George Thorne enjoyed something of a breakthrough season for Albion last year. The graduate of Albion's Academy was recalled from loan at Peterborough United and was thrust straight into the team at Old Trafford just after Christmas, performing well throughout January until his season was cruelly cut short by a knee injury that came in our 2-1 defeat away at Everton. Fully fit again, George will be hoping to push himself back into the Albion reckoning again.

PLAYER PROFILES

SHANE LONG

Birthdate: 22 January 1987
Position: Striker
Height: 1.80m
Weight: 81kg
Other clubs: Reading
Albion games: 51+19
Albion goals: 19

Like James Morrison, Shane enjoyed captaining his country in an international at the end of last season, due reward for another season of never-ending hard work up front for the Baggies. Though Lukaku took a lot of the limelight, Shane's ability and appetite up front were vital to the team, as were his nine Premier League goals, added to three more scored in the cup competitions. A goal against England at Wembley was pretty special, too!

GORAN POPOV

Birthdate: 2 October 1984
Position: Left-back
Height: 1.87m
Weight: 80kg
Other clubs: AEK Athens, Red Star Belgrade, Odra Wodzislaw Slaski, Egaleo, Levadiakos, Heerenveen, Dynamo Kiev
Albion games: 11+2
Albion goals: 0

Goran, a Macedonian international, rejoined the Baggies for a second loan season in the summer of 2013 after spending last season challenging Liam Ridgewell at left-back after making his debut in the 1-1 draw at Villa Park. "Popov the Albion Man", as the supporters know him, is on loan from Ukraine's Dynamo Kiev and will be doing his best to make use of the local knowledge and Premier League experience that he gained during his first year in West Bromwich!

MARKUS ROSENBERG

Birthdate: 27 September 1982
Position: Striker
Height: 1.82m
Weight: 79kg
Other clubs: Malmo, Halmstads, Ajax, Werder Bremen, Racing Santander
Albion games: 8+19
Albion goals: 0

Markus had a difficult introduction to Premier League football last season, when the goalscoring form of Romelu Lukaku and Shane Long meant that he spent a lot of his time watching from the bench and only getting his chance late on in games. But if you take a look at his record all across Europe, you'll soon see that when he does finally get his chance, Markus knows exactly where the back of the net is!

PLAYER PROFILES

SAIDO BERAHINO

Birthdate: 4 August 1993
Position: Striker
Height: 1.80m
Weight: 82kg
Other clubs: Peterborough United, Northampton town, Brentford (all on loan)
Albion games: 0+1
Albion goals: 0

Saido made his Albion debut as a sub in the League Cup win at Yeovil in August 2012, but it was his form in the following pre-season that really pushed him up the Albion pecking order. Getting his chance up front, Saido really excelled and has put himself forward as another option for Steve Clarke this season, as well as earning himself a call up for the England Under-21 squad.

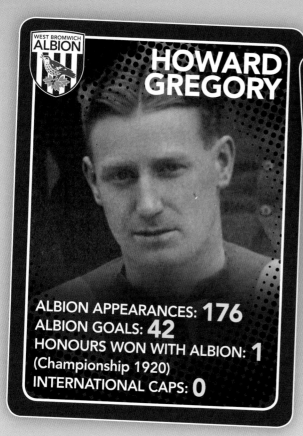

HOWARD GREGORY

ALBION APPEARANCES: **176**
ALBION GOALS: **42**
HONOURS WON WITH ALBION: **1**
(Championship 1920)
INTERNATIONAL CAPS: **0**

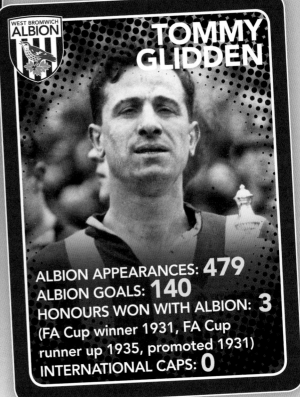

TOMMY GLIDDEN

ALBION APPEARANCES: **479**
ALBION GOALS: **140**
HONOURS WON WITH ALBION: **3**
(FA Cup winner 1931, FA Cup runner up 1935, promoted 1931)
INTERNATIONAL CAPS: **0**

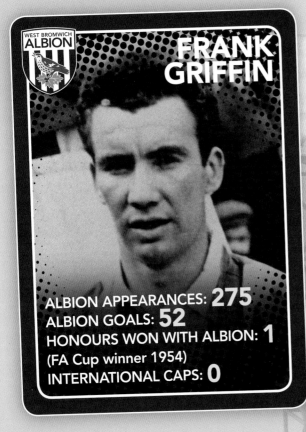

FRANK GRIFFIN

ALBION APPEARANCES: **275**
ALBION GOALS: **52**
HONOURS WON WITH ALBION: **1**
(FA Cup winner 1954)
INTERNATIONAL CAPS: **0**

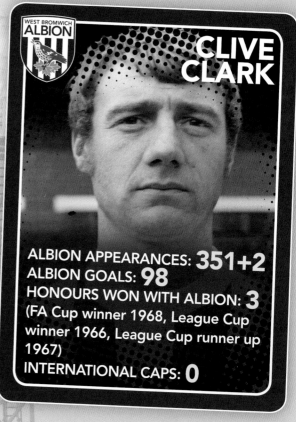

CLIVE CLARK

ALBION APPEARANCES: **351+2**
ALBION GOALS: **98**
HONOURS WON WITH ALBION: **3**
(FA Cup winner 1968, League Cup winner 1966, League Cup runner up 1967)
INTERNATIONAL CAPS: **0**

PLAY YOUR ALBION CARDS RIGHT!
WINGERS

QUIZ & PUZZLE ANSWERS

Page 7 – Maze

Page 30 – Spot the Ball

Page 43 – Wordsearch

T	G	W	X	M	I	A	W	B	A	M
O	D	B	I	L	L	Y	C	B	V	U
N	A	A	L	H	O	F	B	S	S	L
Y	O	F	I	F	Z	F	O	M	F	U
B	R	A	E	O	L	C	Q	C	P	M
R	R	Z	A	N	E	L	K	A	U	B
O	S	M	L	B	D	A	F	U	L	U
W	J	O	B	R	G	R	H	L	Y	P
N	U	S	I	L	D	K	O	E	J	R
R	L	Y	O	O	W	E	X	Y	Z	H
F	J	O	N	A	S	L	A	R	I	E

Pages 36-37 – Big Quiz

1. Brian Little
2. Charlton Athletic
3. Bolton Wanderers
4. Grimsby Town
5. Igor Balis
6. Lee Marshall
7. Kanu
8. Crystal Palace
9. Portsmouth
10. Robert Earnshaw
11. Kevin Phillips
12. Bryan Robson
13. Derby County
14. Paul Peschisolido and Darren Moore
15. Chris Brunt
16. Borja Valero
17. Celtic
18. Roberto di Matteo
19. Doncaster Rovers
20. Graham Dorrans
21. Wolverhampton Wanderers
22. Somen Tchoyi
23. Keith Andrews
24. Ben Foster
25. 17
26. 49

Page 49 – Whose Boots?

1. Liam Ridgewell
2. Izzy Brown
3. Chris Brunt
4. Ben Foster
5. James Morrison
6. Gareth McAuley
7. Youssouf Mulumbu
8. Claudio Yacob